"The Puritan William Gurnall once said, 'Prayer is nothing but the promise reversed or God's word turned inside out and formed into an argument and retorted back again upon God by faith.' It sounds great. But what does it look like in practice? *5 Things to Pray for the People You Love* and *5 Things to Pray for Your Church* answer that question. They'll walk you through using God's word in prayer. And praying God's word is my number one tip to help people invigorate their prayer life. Read these books and invigorate your prayers."

Tim Chester, Pastor of Grace Church, Boroughbridge, and author of *You Can Pray* (IVP)

"*Five Things to Pray* is a brilliantly simple but hugely effective means of stimulating your prayer life for church, mission, family and friends. Accessible and attractive, with lots of Scripture to focus prayer, it will be a great tool for churches to help members to pray regularly and creatively."

Trevor Archer, FIEC London Director

"I recommend this series to you on the basis of the simple fact that they moved me to pray. They both showed me ways to pray for my church and my loved ones, and they kindled in my heart a *want* to pray. These are simple books, with the modest and eternally profound aim of showing how the Bible informs our prayers. Rachel Jones manages to withdraw from the picture and leaves the reader to see how simple it is to align our prayers with the will of our listening Father. These books could well be a cause of great blessing for your church and people you love."

John Hindley, Pastor of BroadGrace Church, Norfolk, and author of *Serving Without Sinking* and *You Can Really Grow*

"For those of us who often struggle to know what to pray for our church and for the people we love, these books are brilliant at giving us lots of really helpful, specific things to pray that are straight from God's word. With a mixture of praise, confession, thanksgiving and petition, the prayers are repeatedly focused on what it looks like to live in the light of eternity in the various different situations that are highlighted. Starting with Scripture really helpfully ensures that we are not praying merely for changed circumstances, as we can tend to do, but rather for changed hearts that bring honour and glory to God."

Andrea Trevenna, Associate Minister for Women at St Nicholas, Sevenoaks, and author of *The Heart of Singleness*

THINGS TO
5
PRAY
FOR YOUR
CHURCH

RACHEL JONES

SERIES EDITOR: CARL LAFERTON

5 things to pray for your church
Prayers that change things for the life of your church

© The Good Book Company, 2016
Reprinted 2016 (twice), 2017 (twice), 2018 (twice), 2019
Series Editor: Carl Laferton

Published by:
The Good Book Company

thegoodbook.com | thegoodbook.co.uk
thegoodbook.com.au | thegoodbook.co.nz | thegoodbook.co.in

ISBN: 9781784980306 | Printed in Denmark by Nørhaven

Design by André Parker

CONTENTS

INTRODUCTION

I wonder if you have ever struggled to believe this famous verse from the Bible:

> *"The prayer of a righteous person is powerful and effective" (James 5 v 16).*

James is telling us that when righteous people pray righteous prayers, things happen. Things change. The prayers of God's people are powerful. But they are not powerful because we are powerful, or because the words we say are somehow magic, but because the Person we pray to is infinitely, unimaginably powerful. And our prayers are effective—not because we are special, or because there is a special formula to use, but because the God we pray to delights to answer our prayers and change the world because of them.

So what is the secret of effective prayer—how can you pray prayers that really change things? James suggests two questions that we need to ask ourselves.

First, are you righteous? A righteous person is some-one who is in right relationship with God—someone who, through faith in Jesus, has been forgiven and accepted as a child of God. Are you someone who, as you pray, is praying not just to your Maker, not just to your Ruler, but to your heavenly Father, who has completely forgiven you through Jesus?

Second, do your prayers reflect that relationship? If we know God is our Maker, our Ruler and our Father, we will want to pray prayers that please him, that reflect his desires, that line up with his priorities for our lives and for the world. The kind of prayer that truly changes things is the prayer offered by a child of God that reflects God's heart.

That's why, when God's children pray in the Bible, we so often find them using the word of God to guide their prayers. So when Jonah prayed in the belly of a fish to thank God for rescuing him (Jonah 2 v 1-9), he used the words of several psalms strung together. When the first Christians gathered in Jerusalem to pray, they used the themes of Psalm 2 to guide their praise and their requests (Acts 4 v 24-30). And when Paul prayed that his friends would grow in love (Philippians 1 v 9), he was asking the Father to work in them the same thing the Lord Jesus prayed for us (John 17 v 25-26), and which the Holy Spirit is doing for all believers (Romans 5 v 5). They all used God's words to guide their words to God.

How can you pray prayers that are powerful and effective—that change things, that make things happen? First, by being a child of God. Second, by praying Bible prayers, which use God's words to make sure your prayers are pleasing to him and share his priorities.

That's what this little book is here to help you with. It contains suggestions for how to pray for 21 different aspects of church life. And for each of them you'll find guidance for what we can pray—for leaders, for children, for those who are seeking, for faithful preaching, for loving community, for bold evangelism, and much more. Each prayer suggestion is based on a passage of the Bible, so you can be certain that they are prayers that God wants you to pray for your church family.

There are five different suggestions for each. So you can use this book in a variety of ways.

- *You can pray a prayer each day for your church family, over the course of three weeks, and then start again.*

- *You can take one of the prayer themes and pray a part of it every day from Monday to Friday.*

- *Or you can dip in and out of it, as and when you want and need to pray for a particular area of church life.*

- *There's also a space on each page for you to write in the names of specific church members you intend to remember in prayer.*

This is by no means an exhaustive guide—there are plenty more things that you can be praying for your church! But you can be confident as you use it that you are praying great prayers—prayers that God wants you to pray. And God promises that "the prayer of a righteous person is powerful and effective". That's a promise that is worth grasping hold of confidently. As we pray trusting this promise, it will change how we pray and what we expect to come from our prayers.

THAT MY CHURCH WOULD...

REMEMBER
WHAT WE ARE

1 PETER 2 v 9-10

PEOPLE TO PRAY FOR:

_____

_____

_____

_____

Help my church family to remember that we are...

 ## A HOLY NATION

"But you are a chosen people ... a holy nation" (v 9).

Thank God that he has chosen to show his wonderful grace to you and your church family. Thank God that those who are in Christ are new creations—a whole new "race" (or nation) of people. Pray that members of your church would increasingly act like the holy people God has declared you to be.

 ## A ROYAL PRIESTHOOD

Thank God for the job title that he has given his chosen people: "priests".

Like the Old Testament priests, we're to represent people before God and represent God before people. Ask that your church would be faithful in praying for those inside and outside of your community. And pray that you'd be faithful in speaking and applying God's word into the lives of those around you.

GOD'S SPECIAL POSSESSION

Thank God that he has made your church his "special possession" (v 9).

Thank him that you can be assured of his love, whatever life throws at you. Pray that this would give your church a great sense of security and confidence—pray that you would not fear what others might think of you or do to you.

CALLED

Thank God that he has called each member of your church "out of darkness into his wonderful light" (v 9).

Take a few moments to thank God for the way in which he called some specific people you know. Pray that your church would increasingly "declare the praises" of God by living distinctively and speaking the good news boldly.

RECIPIENTS OF MERCY

Thank God that though "once you had not received mercy … now you have received mercy" (v 10).

Pray that your church would grow in your appreciation of the depth of God's mercy—and that this would crush any lingering feelings of self-righteousness. Pray that you'd show mercy to each other—forgiving the small things, the big things, and the things that seem to happen again and again.

THAT MY CHURCH WOULD...

BE A BODY GROWING IN MATURITY

EPHESIANS 4 v 11-16

PEOPLE TO PRAY FOR:

_____

_____

_____

_____

Father God, help us to...

BE EQUIPPED

Thank God for the leaders that "Christ him-self" has given your church, "to equip his people for works of service..." (v 11-12).

Pray that your church (and your leaders) would see your leaders in the same way that Paul does—not there to do everything themselves, but to equip all of Christ's people to do his work. Ask God to give your leaders wisdom in discerning the areas where members need equipping most, and how best they can do that.

BE UNITED

"... until we all reach unity" (v 13).

Pray that your church's unity would not come from being similar types of people in the first place, but that it would be a deeper kind: "unity in the faith and in the knowledge of the Son of God". Thank God that through the gospel, such unity is possible!

BECOME MATURE

Pray that your church would be growing more and more into "the mature body of him who is the head, that is, Christ" (v 15).

Pray that your family would grow "in every respect"— in each area of believers' lives.

 BE STEADFAST

Pray that your church would not be "tossed back and forth by the waves" (v 14).

What difficult circumstances are threatening to unsettle individuals in your church? What biblical teachings are you tempted to compromise on? Pray that your church would hold steadfastly to the truth. Pray that every member—whether they're preaching from the front, contributing at a Bible study or chatting over coffee— would remain confident in the truths of God's word.

 BUILD EACH OTHER UP

Ask God to help your church "grow" and "build" one another up (v 16).

Ask God to give you specific opportunities to do so when you next meet with your church family! Pray that you would not flinch from speaking hard truth to one another, but that you would do so "in love". Thank God that it is "by every supporting ligament" that the church grows, "as each part does its work". Pray that those who are on the fringes of church life would come to see the essential role they can play.

THINGS TO PRAY

THAT MY CHURCH WOULD...

BE DEVOTED TO ONE ANOTHER

ACTS 2 v 42-47

PEOPLE TO PRAY FOR:

_____

_____

_____

_____

Heavenly Father, help us to be devoted to...

LEARNING TOGETHER

Thank God that he has given the church "the apostles' teaching" in the pages of Scripture (v 42).

Pray that your church would be devoted to learning from it together—whether that's in Sunday services, Bible-study groups, or one to one. Pray that you would be committed to attending, even at the end of a draining day or hectic week. And pray that your hearts and minds would be engaged and stirred by God's word as you meet week by week.

BUILDING RELATIONSHIPS

*"They devoted themselves ... to fellowship ...
All the believers were together" (v 42, 44).*

Ask that your church would also be devoted to spending the time together required to forge meaningful relationships. Thank God for the friendships you already have at church; then prayerfully think about who else you could seek to deepen your relationship with this month.

PRAYING TOGETHER

"They devoted themselves ... to prayer"
(v 42).

It's sometimes said that a church's prayer meetings are like a spiritual barometer. So what's the reading on your church's barometer? Ask that a culture of prayer would permeate your church, and that God would make you into people who delight in coming together to pray.

MEETING NEEDS...

The first believers "sold property and possessions to give to anyone who had need" (v 45).

Pray that your church would also be sacrificial in your generosity—always ready to meet each other's material, emotional and spiritual needs. Pray that you would be willing to give up your time, money or convenience to ensure that others have what they need.

... AND ADD TO OUR NUMBER

Thank God for the people and families he's "added to [your] number" recently (v 47).

Pray that your church would be a community that is friendly and welcoming to newcomers. Pray that your church would grow: that people would come to your gatherings, be introduced to Jesus, see him at work in the lives of his people and put their faith in his saving work.

THAT MY CHURCH WOULD...

LOVE AND SERVE
ONE ANOTHER

1 CORINTHIANS 13 v 4-7

PEOPLE TO PRAY FOR:

_____

_____

_____

_____

Lord, help us to love one another in a way that...

IS PATIENT AND KIND

"Love is patient, love is kind" (v 4).

Thank God for being patient with your church. For all your failings, he continues to treasure you! Pray that your church would love one another with the same patience—that you wouldn't get annoyed when people seem slow to change or don't do things the way you'd like. Pray that your love would overflow in acts of kindness towards each other.

ISN'T PROUD OR SELF-SEEKING

"It is not proud ... it is not self-seeking" (v 4-5).

Pray that as a church, you'd love one another with Christ-like humility: willing to do the jobs that are dirty, difficult or dull; willing to associate with people who seem needy, frustrating or just a bit odd. Pray that each of you wouldn't seek your own benefit or enjoyment, but would do things for the benefit of others.

KEEPS NO RECORD OF WRONGS

"It keeps no record of wrongs" (v 5).

You're going to hurt others, let them down, and make bad decisions—and your brothers and sisters in Christ will do that to you too. Thank God that he keeps no record of your wrongs; pray that as a church, you wouldn't either. Ask for grace to repent quickly, forgive quickly and move on quickly.

 REJOICES WITH THE TRUTH

Spend some time rejoicing over the people in your church that God has recently brought to trust in the saving truth of the gospel (v 6).

Or think of some of your brothers and sisters who have grown in their knowledge of the truth, and how that's been changing their lives—then rejoice! Pray that your church would be one that is always rejoicing in the truth.

 TRUSTS, HOPES, PERSEVERES

Pray that God would form you into a community that "always trusts, always hopes, always perseveres" (v 7).

Pray that you'd trust one another enough to be real with each other; that your hopes would become one another's hopes, as you desire the best for each other; that your relationships would last for the long haul, as your love perseveres through good and bad times.

THAT MY CHURCH WOULD...

HOLD TO
THE TRUTH

PSALM 19 v 7-13

PEOPLE TO PRAY FOR:

Almighty Father, help us to be a church which regards your word as…

 PERFECT

> *"The law of the LORD is perfect, refreshing the soul" (v 7).*

Thank God that he has not left us guessing, but has provided his perfect, trustworthy word so that we can truly know him. Pray that as your church gathers around the Bible, you would have your souls refreshed as you encounter the living God.

 RADIANT

> *Thank God that his radiant word gives "light to the eyes" (v 8).*

Thank him that by the power of the Holy Spirit, the pages of Scripture show us who Jesus is and what he has done. It is by being taught the truths from God's radiant word that people are changed—so pray that teachers in your church would remember this. Ask God to use their words this week to enlighten many eyes.

FIRM

In a world where the moral goalposts seem to shift often, thank God that his words "are firm, and all of them are righteous" (v 9).

Pray that your church would not compromise with culture—perhaps there are specific areas where you are particularly feeling the pressure at the moment. Pray that you'd all firmly hold that what the Bible says is right and wise really is right and wise.

 SWEET

God's decrees are "sweeter than honey, than honey from the honeycomb" (v 10).

Consider what it is that you most love to eat—then pray that your church would love feeding on God's word more than you love feeding on that food! Pray that learning from Scripture wouldn't be a dry, academic exercise, but a delightful, sweet treat.

 A WARNING

The psalmist asks, "Who can discern their own errors?" (v 12).

Pray that your church wouldn't go out from meeting together and ignore—or forget—what you've heard. Instead, pray that the warnings from God's word would change how you live (v 11). Pray that Scripture would be showing you your hidden faults and turning you from sin, so that every one of you "will be blameless, innocent of great transgression".

THAT MY CHURCH WOULD...

MAKE KNOWN GOD'S GLORY

ROMANS 1 v 14-17

PEOPLE TO PRAY FOR:

_____

_____

_____

_____

Father, in our evangelism, help us to...

FEEL INDEBTED

"I am a debtor..." (v 14).

Sometimes people feel that evangelism is something best left to the "experts" or church leaders. But we've been given so much in the gospel of Jesus Christ that every Christian is indebted and obligated to share it. Pray that every member of your church would feel that burden to proclaim the gospel—shaking off apathy and being filled with compassion for the lost.

REACH DIVERSE GROUPS

"... both to Greeks and non-Greeks, both to the wise and the foolish" (v 14).

Pray that your church would reach diverse groups of people within your community. We all tend to gravitate towards people who are like us; but pray that your church would be able to push outside their comfort zone. What would that look like in your situation? Pray that you'd warmly embrace all types of people, confident that the gospel can transform all types of people.

BE EAGER

"I am so eager to preach the gospel" (v 15).

Very often our evangelistic efforts leave us feeling guilty and awkward. Pray that your church would share Paul's joy and eagerness at the prospect of preaching the gospel.

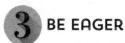 **BE CONFIDENT**

"I am not ashamed of the gospel" (v 16).

Pray for boldness as your church disperses each week to your individual homes, neighbourhoods and workplaces; that you would unashamedly seek opportunities to share the gospel. Perhaps this is a season of discouragement for some in your church; pray that even when people seem to respond with indifference, you would remain confident that the gospel is both *good* and *powerful*—powerful enough to bring "salvation to everyone who believes" (v 16).

 MARVEL AT THE GOSPEL

Take a few moments to marvel at verse 17: "In the gospel the righteousness of God is revealed—a righteousness that is by faith from first to last".

Thank God that through faith in the gospel, you have been made righteous; and thank God for making your brothers and sisters in Christ righteous too. Pray that as a church, you would never stop marvelling at God's incredible grace to you.

THAT MY CHURCH WOULD...

GIVE
GENEROUSLY

2 CORINTHIANS 9 v 6-15

PEOPLE TO PRAY FOR:

_____

_____

_____

_____

Lord, as we give to your work, help us to...

GIVE CHEERFULLY

"God loves a cheerful giver" (v 7)—so pray that your church would be full of them!

Pray that people in your church would not give "reluctantly or under compulsion", but joyfully, out of gratitude for all God has given them. Pray that a culture of cheerful giving would take root in your church: that you would give generously not just to the church itself, but also directly to one another as needs arise.

ABOUND IN GOOD WORKS

"You will abound in every good work" (v 8).

Many people have a lot more money than time. So pray that members would also be willing to give generously of their time and effort to serve your church family, both in formal and more informal ways. Thank God for those who are already abounding in good works; pray that more volunteers would step up for ministries that need them; and ask God to encourage the weary servants you know.

GROW IN RIGHTEOUSNESS

> *"He ... will enlarge the harvest of your righteousness" (v 10).*

As we give, we have the opportunity to grow more like our generous heavenly Father. Pray that your church would have the right perspective on their giving: not as merely a way to keep the building's lights on, but as an exciting opportunity to "enlarge the harvest of your righteousness".

 POINT PEOPLE TO CHRIST

> *"Others will praise God for the obedience that accompanies your confession of the gospel of Christ" (v 13).*

Praise God for the obedient giving that the gospel has brought about in your church. Then pray for those responsible for spending this money, asking that it would be spent wisely, for gospel purposes. Pray that as these resources enable more people to hear the good news, those people would believe it and in turn praise God too! Pray for some specific people or projects that your church supports financially.

 THANK GOD...

> *"... for his indescribable gift!" (v 15).*

Nothing we give can compare to the wonderful riches God has given us in his Son; thank him now.

THINGS TO
PRAY

5

THAT I WOULD...

USE MY
GIFTS WELL

ROMANS 12 v 1-9

PEOPLE TO PRAY FOR:

_____

_____

_____

_____

Father God, please help me to...

SERVE SACRIFICIALLY

We're to serve others "in view of God's mercy" (v 1)—motivated by the grace he has shown to us.

Spend some time reflecting on and thanking God for his mercy. Then pray that you'd offer the whole of your life as an act of "true and proper worship" in response to what he's done for you—serving at great cost to yourself, just as God gave so much to you at the great cost of his own Son.

SERVE HUMBLY

Paul is unequivocal: "Do not think of yourself more highly than you ought" (v 3).

Yet so often, exercising our gifts leads to feelings of pride, however secret: *I could have taught that better than him; I'm way more committed than she is; My talent's being wasted on this job.* Confess your sin to God and ask him to root out your pride and grow you in humility.

VALUE THE GIFTS OF OTHERS

Thank God for the wonderful diversity of his church: a body "with many members" where we all "have different gifts" (v 4-6).

Think about some specific people in your church, and thank God for the way he's equipped them to serve his people. Pray that you'd value the talents and skills of others: that you'd remember to show your appreciation and encourage them to use those gifts well.

 USE MY GIFTS

"If your gift is prophesying, then prophesy … if it is serving, then serve..." (v 6-7).

God has given us gifts so that we can use them. Ask God to show you whether you're using the gifts he's given you well (whether that's your skills or your money, v 8). Thank our Father for the opportunities you have to serve your church. Pray that you'd serve with the right attitude—never grudgingly, but diligently and cheerfully (v 8).

 LOVE SINCERELY

"Love must be sincere" (v 9).

Sometimes we serve so that people will love us (or at least like and respect us). But pray that you'd serve as an expression of genuine love towards others—whatever it is you're doing. Pray that your love would "be sincere": that as you love others by serving them practically, you'd be loving them from the heart too.

THAT I WOULD...

PERSEVERE WHEN I GET WEARY

HEBREWS 10 v 19-25

PEOPLE TO PRAY FOR:

_____

_____

_____

_____

Father, when I'm feeling weary, help me to...

THANK YOU

"We have confidence to enter the Most Holy Place by the blood of Jesus" (v 19).

Coming together to worship God with our church family can sometimes feel like a chore. But these verses remind us that it's a privilege that was hard-won by the blood of Jesus. Thank Christ that he has opened up a way into relationship with God through his death (v 20).

DRAW NEAR TO YOU

"Let us draw near to God..." (v 22).

Often a guilty conscience or a feeling of inadequacy makes us want to run a mile from other Christians. Thank God that Christ's death and resurrection has the power to completely "cleanse us". Thank God that you can draw near to him "with the full assurance that faith brings" (v 22). Pray that next time you mess up, you would be quick to repent and receive forgiveness, and be restored to your church family.

HOLD ON UNSWERVINGLY

Sometimes it's doubts that leave us wanting to avoid church; pray that you would "hold unswervingly to the hope [you] profess" by trusting God's unchanging character (v 23).

Thank God that he is "faithful"—even when his people are not. Pray that you'd remember and hold on to his faithfulness when others let you down.

 ## SPUR OTHERS ON

Hebrews tells us to "consider how we may spur one another on towards love and good deeds" (v 24). Consider that now!

Ask God to renew your attitude so that you meet with your church family not to be entertained or only to be fed with God's word, but with the intention of spurring others on. Or perhaps you feel that you're doing lots to little effect; ask God to use your words and example to bear fruit in the lives of others.

 ## NEVER GIVE UP

"Not giving up meeting together…" (v 25).

Sometimes when we're weary, we turn up at church physically, but disengage from others spiritually and emotionally. Ask God to help you not give up truly "meeting" with others; and that as you engage, you would be encouraged. Thank God that "the Day" is approaching when fellowship with his people will never feel wearying! Ask him to keep you going until then.

5 THINGS TO PRAY

THAT I WOULD...

BE WHO MY FAMILY NEEDS ME TO BE

EPHESIANS 4 v 1-6

PEOPLE TO PRAY FOR:

_____

_____

_____

_____

THANK GOD

Thank God that he has called you to be one of his people (v 1).

The first three chapters of Ephesians richly describe how amazing this calling is. We have been called to "adoption to sonship through Jesus Christ" (1 v 5). We have "redemption through his blood, the forgiveness of sins" (1 v 7); "the promised Holy Spirit ... guaranteeing our inheritance" (1 v 13); and "access to the Father" (2 v 18). He loves us with a "love that surpasses knowledge" (3 v 19)! Praise and thank God for each of these wonderful truths. *Then pray that you would "live a life worthy of [this] calling" by...*

BEING COMPLETELY HUMBLE

Paul tells us to "be completely humble" (4 v 2)—just appearing humble won't cut it.

Pray that as you look to Christ's humility, the Holy Spirit would make your heart more and more like his. Pray that this would work its way out in the things you do and the way you treat people at church.

BEING COMPLETELY GENTLE

Ask for help to be "completely ... gentle" in your actions, thoughts and words.

Pray that God would prevent you from hurting your brothers and sisters with harsh, cutting or thoughtless words. Pray that you would be sensitive to the needs of others, and kind in seeking to meet them.

 BEING PATIENT

"Be patient, bearing with one another in love" (v 2).

When do you find it most difficult to be patient with your church family? When someone on your team turns up late again? When that guy in your home group makes another uncaring remark? When that person you're mentoring messes up again? Pray that you would bear with others "in love"—not through gritted teeth.

 STAYING UNITED

Ask God to help you "make every effort" to keep "the bond of peace" when disagreements arise (v 3).

Thank God that your church family has something deeper in common than any other community: you are one body which shares the same faith and the same heavenly Father. "You were called to one hope" (v 4)—so pray that your church family would be united as you work towards your common goal.

FOR...

MY CHURCH
LEADER

MALACHI 2 v 5-6

PEOPLE TO PRAY FOR:

_____

_____

_____

_____

THANK GOD

Thank God for the "covenant of life and peace" he has made with this person (v 5).

Thank God that through the new covenant of Christ's blood, your leader is at peace with him and has been given the gift of eternal life. Thank God for the way that, in view of the gospel, your leader gives their time, effort and talents in the service of your church.

Then pray that your church leader would...

REVERE GOD

"He revered me and stood in awe of my name" (v 5).

Praise God for his awesome, majestic holiness and power. Pray that your leader would daily be reminded of this side of God's character in their times of private prayer and Bible reading. It's easy for the grind of day-to-day ministry to become motivated by a fear of people or a desire to please others; but pray that your church leader would always stand "in awe of [God's] name" (v 5).

WALK UPRIGHTLY

"He walked with me in peace and upright-ness" (v 6).

Our church leaders are not immune to temptation; in fact, ministry brings its own set of challenges. So pray that your leader would walk uprightly. Ask God to give them strength in their daily fight against sin, and enable them to lead with humility, love, patience and gentleness. Pray that they'd walk uprightly in their family life too.

 GIVE TRUE INSTRUCTION

Pray that as this leader preaches and teaches, "true instruction [would be] in his mouth and nothing false [would be] found on his lips" (v 6).

Thank God for the ways you've benefitted from your leader's instruction. Pray for your leader as they counsel individuals—that God would be filling their mouth with true instruction at these times too.

 TURN MANY FROM SIN

"He ... turned many from sin" (v 6).

Pray that your leader wouldn't shy away from lovingly calling people to turn from their sin. Instead, ask that their "true instruction" would be fruitful in "turning many from sin": for fruitful discipleship as church members grow in maturity; and for fruitful evangelism as people repent and believe the gospel.

FOR...

MY SMALL
GROUP

COLOSSIANS 3 v 15-17

PEOPLE TO PRAY FOR:

_____

_____

_____

_____

Heavenly Father, please help us to...

 BE AT PEACE

> *"Let the peace of Christ rule in your hearts" (v 15).*

This is more than the absence of arguing! Thank God that your small group are all "members of one body", knit together as part of Christ's body (v 15). Yet all of us have at some point had mean thoughts, angry attitudes and bitter motives in our hearts, however well we cover them up. Repent before God, and ask that Christ's peace would rule in your heart instead.

 TEACH ONE ANOTHER

> *"Let the message of Christ dwell among you richly as you teach ... one another" (v 16).*

Pray that during your small-group Bible studies, you would not only learn together, but also revel in the glorious riches of the message of Christ. Thank God that small groups also give an opportunity to learn from the wisdom of people at different life-stages. Pray that all of you would be willing to listen and learn.

ADMONISH ONE ANOTHER

Small groups should be an environment where Christians can "admonish" one another (v 16).

Pray for a group culture of intimacy and honesty; that as you share your lives together, you would hold each other accountable, lovingly point out sin, and earnestly warn one another against wrongdoing. This is hard; but pray you would love one another enough to have these difficult conversations.

 ## LOVE EACH OTHER...

... both in "word" and "deed" (v 17).

Pray that you wouldn't be a group that just meets once a week to talk about the Bible, but a group that truly loves each other with words and deeds at other times too. Then think of a way you can put this prayer point into action!

 ## BE TRULY THANKFUL

See verses 15, 16 and 17!

Paul tells the Colossians three times in as many verses to be thankful. So as you think of your small group, think of three things you can be grateful for; then thank God for them!

FOR...

CHILDREN IN MY CHURCH

PSALM 78 v 1-7

PEOPLE TO PRAY FOR:

_____

_____

_____

_____

 GIVE THANKS

Give thanks for "the praiseworthy deeds of the LORD" (v 4).

Think of the Bible story that you loved most as a child or new believer; thank God for what he did in history, and for the fact that now, thousands of years later, you "have heard and known" about it. Praise God for "his power, and the wonders he has done"—especially his wonderful work of rescuing sinners through the death and resurrection of Jesus.

 WHOLE-CHURCH INVOLVEMENT

"We will tell the next generation the praiseworthy deeds of the LORD" (v 4).

Notice the word "we"; sharing God's praiseworthy deeds with children is a responsibility for all of God's people. Pray that your church would be a nurturing family where every child has lots of spiritual "aunts and uncles" committed to their growth. Pray for opportunities to invest meaningfully in the lives of children at your church.

FAITHFUL BIBLE-TEACHING

"[The LORD] decreed statutes for Jacob ... which he commanded our ancestors to teach their children" (v 5).

Pray for those particularly involved in teaching the Bible to children—for parents as well as leaders. Pray for some of these individuals by name, that they would teach the Bible faithfully and clearly, and model what it looks like to obey God's commands.

TRUST IN GOD

Pray that the children of your church would "put their trust in God" (v 7).

No amount of Sunday-school lessons or Bible-club sessions can make a child a Christian—this only happens by God's grace. So ask him now that children in your church would "put their trust in God". Spend some time praying this for specific children you know.

FRUIT FOR YEARS TO COME

Pray that the children would "not forget [God's] deeds" as they grow up, but that they'd continue to walk with Jesus (v 7).

Pray that what they learn now would be laying the groundwork for a mature faith in adulthood. Look ahead 30 years and pray that one day, these children "in turn would tell their children" (v 6). Pray that keeping a long-term perspective would guard parents and leaders from discouragement.

FOR...

OUR YOUNG PEOPLE

1 TIMOTHY 4 v 10-13

PEOPLE TO PRAY FOR:

_____

_____

_____

_____

THANK THE LIVING GOD

Praise God that he is "the living God, who is the Saviour of all people, and especially of those who believe" (v 10).

Thank him that all who put their hope in him will never be disappointed. Pray that parents and leaders who work with young people would be able to echo Paul in saying that this, above anything else, "is why we labour and strive".

Pray that your teenagers would set an example in...

LOVE

"Set an example ... in love" (v 12).

Pray that young people would grow in their understanding of God's love for them—and that this would result in a growing love for him and the people around them. If your church has a youth group, pray especially that this would be a gracious community where every person loves and is loved, regardless of whatever differences there might be between them.

3 FAITH

Pray that God would bring many young people to a saving faith in Christ (v 12).

Thank God for those he already has saved. Pray that this would be a faith that lasts: that your teenagers wouldn't give up and drop off from church, but persevere in following Christ right into adulthood.

4 SPEECH, CONDUCT AND PURITY

Pray that the faith your young people profess on Sundays would be worked out in the way they act and speak on every other day of the week (v 12).

Ask God to strengthen them to resist the temptations they face at home and school. Especially pray for resolve to pursue sexual purity.

5 DEVOTION TO SCRIPTURE

"Devote yourself to the ... reading of Scripture, to preaching and to teaching" (v 13).

How will points 2 – 4 happen? As God speaks to young people through his word. Pray that the Holy Spirit would be working in the hearts of teenagers as they study his word in their groups, hear it preached as part of the wider church, and read it on their own. Pray that the young people of your fellowship would be "devoted" to reading Scripture—not out of habit, guilt or parental compulsion, but because they love walking closely with their heavenly Father.

FOR...

NOT-YET
CHRISTIANS

ACTS 17 v 10-12

PEOPLE TO PRAY FOR:

_____

_____

_____

_____

*You could use this to pray for an individual or family,
or for a forthcoming evangelistic event. Pray for...*

WHOLE-CHURCH SUPPORT

> *"The believers sent Paul and Silas away to
> Berea" (v 10).*

Pray that sharing the gospel wouldn't be something
that's left to a few keen lone-ranger evangelists, but
something that has the backing and active involvement of the whole fellowship. Pray that everyone in
your church would see the need to devote money,
time and talents to evangelism.

AN EAGER RECEPTION

> *Pray that like the Bereans, not-yet-Chris-
> tians would "[receive] the message with
> great eagerness" (v 11).*

Ask God to prepare their hearts for the message: to
remove stumbling blocks and grow in them a spiritual
hunger. Pray that seeing people respond to the gospel with curiosity, excitement and joy would encourage your church.

EXAMINING THE SCRIPTURES

*"They ... examined the Scriptures every day
to see if what Paul said was true" (v 11).*

Faith that's built on the strength of someone's per-
sonality or the charisma of their preaching will not
last. But God's word is truly powerful. Pray that as
non-believers encounter Christ in the pages of Scripture, they'd be compelled by the historical evidence
and drawn by his character.

 MANY TO BELIEVE

"As a result, many of them believed" (v 12).

Ask plainly and simply that many who hear the good
news about Jesus at your church would believe it.

 DIVERSITY

*In Berea, many Jews became believers,
"as did also a number of prominent Greek
women and many Greek men" (v 12).*

Thank God that he welcomes all kinds of people into
his family; pray that your church would too. Praise
God that the gospel message has the power to save
anyone, no matter what his or her background is.
Thank God for some of the "unlikely converts" that
are already part of your church; pray that he would
bring many more.

FOR...

MERCY
MINISTRIES

ACTS 6 v 1-7

PEOPLE TO PRAY FOR:

Lift this ministry before the Lord and ask that it would...

 ## DELIVER JUSTICE

"Their widows were being overlooked..."
(v 1).

We serve a God who hates injustice, oppression, division and poverty; praise God for this aspect of his character! Thank God that this particular ministry plays a part in his big plan to make the world right again. Pray that it would be effective in delivering justice to the marginalised and help to the suffering.

 ## BE FULL OF THE SPIRIT

"Choose seven men from among you who are known to be full of the Spirit..." (v 3).

Pray that the Christians involved in this ministry would carry out their work with love, joy, patience, kindness and self-control. This can only be done by the Holy Spirit! Ask God to generously pour his Spirit into the hearts of those involved.

BE FULL OF WISDOM

"... and wisdom" (v 3).

The leaders of this ministry will regularly face a mine-field of hard decisions. Perhaps they're big decisions about the direction the ministry is taking; perhaps they're smaller decisions about what to say to a difficult person. In either case, your brothers and sisters need wisdom in this work; ask God to give it to them.

 HAVE WHOLE-CHURCH SUPPORT

"This proposal pleased the whole group ... They presented these men to the apostles, who prayed and laid their hands on them" (v 5-6).

In this passage we see "word" ministry and practical ministries complementing each other; pray that this would be the case in your church too. Pray that practical ministry would be valued and supported by your whole church—think about specific ways you can offer your encouragement.

 SPREAD THE WORD

"So the word of God spread" (v 7).

Thank God that Christians don't just offer temporary solutions to human suffering, but an eternal one too. Pray for opportunities to share the gospel through this work. Pray that as non-Christians see God's people treating them with compassion and love, they'd be drawn to our compassionate, loving God.

FOR...

THE ELDERLY

JOSHUA 14 v 6-15

PEOPLE TO PRAY FOR:

_____

_____

_____

_____

 ### THANK GOD

"I was forty years old when..." (v 7).

Thank God for the ways the older folk in your church have served him and blessed his people over the years. Just like Caleb, who had to remind the Israelites of his role in exploring the promised land (v 6-9), elderly members of your church have probably done more than most can remember! But thank God that he has seen every detail of their years of faithful service.

 ### STRENGTH AND VIGOUR

"Here I am today, eighty-five years old! I am still as strong today ... I'm just as vigorous" (v 10-11).

Old age may slow us down in many ways, but pray that the older folk in your church would stay spiritually strong and vigorous. Especially bring before God any individuals who are feeling worn down from illness or infirmity. Pray that in spite of physical suffering, they'd share Caleb's eagerness to serve God and share stories of his faithfulness.

CONFIDENCE IN GOD

"Just as the LORD promised, he has…" (v 10).

Pray that like Caleb, the elderly in your church would be excited and encouraged as they look back on how God has fulfilled his promises to them. Pray that they would have great confidence that, with "the LORD helping" them (v 12), they will one day be brought through to the better promised land—the wonderful heavenly country.

BLESSED BY THE CHURCH

"Then Joshua blessed Caleb" (v 13).

Thank God for the people who are especially seeking to meet the needs of elderly people in your church: the people who give them lifts, bring them a cup of coffee after the service, and invite them over for Christmas. Often the care of older people falls to a select few, but pray that everyone in your church would seek to bless your elderly members. Prayerfully think through how that might look for you.

LISTENED TO AND VALUED

"So Hebron … belonged to Caleb" (v 14).

After Caleb had spoken, they acted on what he said! Pray that your church would seek, listen to and act on the wisdom of older members. Pray that older folk would feel increasingly loved and valued as they fulfil their vital role as spiritual mothers and fathers in the family of God.

FOR...

ANOTHER CHURCH NEAR US

PHILIPPIANS 1 v 3-11

PEOPLE TO PRAY FOR:

_____

_____

_____

_____

Bring another church in your area or network before God and pray...

THANKING GOD FOR THIS CHURCH

Thank God for this church's "partnership in the gospel" (v 4).

"Pray with joy", thanking God that he has begun "a good work" in believers there by bringing them to faith in Christ. This is nothing less than a miracle, so praise God!

THANKING GOD FOR YOUR SHARED GRACE

Thank God that though your churches may look and feel very different, "you share in God's grace" (v 7).

Thank God for the link between your two congregations. Pray that there'd be no hint of rivalry or jealousy between you, but only increasing affection (v 8).

FOR ABOUNDING LOVE

Pray that this church's "love may abound more and more in knowledge and depth of insight" (v 9).

Pray that God would fill them with an abounding love for him, an abounding love for one another, and an abounding love for the lost. Pray too that they'd grow in their knowledge of God as they look at his word.

FOR DISCERNMENT

Pray for discernment on an individual level; that each day members of this church would be choosing to do what is "pure and blameless" (v 10).

Then pray for discernment on a whole-church level. What difficult situations or decisions are they facing? Pray that this church would know the best way ahead, "to the glory and praise of God" (v 11).

FOR RIGHTEOUS FRUIT

Pray that this church would be "filled with the fruit of righteousness that comes through Jesus Christ" (v 11).

Pray that nobody would fall for the lie that we can be made right with God by going to church and being nice to people. Instead, pray that this church would grow as more people come along, hear the gospel and become right with God through faith in Christ.

FOR...

OUR MISSION
PARTNER

1 THESSALONIANS 2 v 1-12

PEOPLE TO PRAY FOR:

_____

_____

_____

 THANK GOD

Thank God for the New Testament missionaries like Paul; for their "toil and hardship" in growing the early church (v 9).

Then thank God for your mission partner. Thank God for his grace in saving them; thank God for the gifts and talents he's given them; thank God for their willingness to use these talents to serve him cross-culturally.

 ENCOURAGEMENT

"We are not trying to please people but God, who tests our hearts" (v 4).

Serving God cross-culturally can bring a barrage of discouragements: health problems, difficult team relationships, spiritual attack or a seeming lack of fruit. Pray that your mission partner would be encouraged, knowing that they are not trying to please local partners or their sending church, but God—and that their continued faithfulness is what delights their Father.

FOCUSED ON THE GOSPEL

> *"With the help of our God we dared to tell you his gospel in the face of strong opposition" (v 2).*

Your mission partner might work in a part of the world where sharing the gospel carries significant risk. Ask God for courage. Your mission partner may also have a "secular" job, which can threaten to steal focus, energy and time from this primary goal. Pray that, as in Paul's case, this "tent-making" would facilitate gospel ministry, rather than distract from it.

 WALKING RIGHTEOUSLY

> *Pray that this missionary would live in a way that is "holy, righteous and blameless" (v 10), even when things are hard.*

Perhaps you know some ways in which this person struggles to be godly; pray through these specifically.

 DEEPENING RELATIONSHIPS

> *Pray that, like Paul, your mission partner would be always "encouraging, comforting and urging [local Christians] to live lives worthy of God" (v 12).*

Thank God for the Christians—your brothers and sisters!—in this part of the world. Pray that your mission partner would be able to grow deep relationships with local believers, built on a unity in the gospel that overcomes all cultural differences.

FOR...

CHURCHES
FAR AWAY

1 PETER 4 v 12-19

PEOPLE TO PRAY FOR:

_____

_____

_____

_____

You could pray this for a specific partner church in another country; or for churches facing persecution.

REJOICE IN SUFFERING

If this church faces persecution, pray that they'd "rejoice inasmuch as [they] participate in the sufferings of Christ" (v 13).

Pray that they wouldn't be surprised by suffering, but confident in Christ's love for them, knowing that he suffered on behalf of all his people so that one day we will suffer no more. Wherever this church is, they'll definitely be suffering from the general effects of the fall: illness, pain, relational conflict, and so on. Pray that, no matter how bad they feel, these Christians would remember that they are "blessed" because "the Spirit of glory" rests on them (v 14).

LOOK FORWARD

Thank God that we will "be overjoyed when [Christ's] glory is revealed" (v 14).

Pray that this church would be looking forward more and more to that day, and living in the truth of it.

NOT BE ASHAMED

Take a moment to "praise God that you bear that name" of "Christian"—a name you share with millions around the world (v 16)!

Pray that churches in other parts of the world would "not be ashamed" to be one of the Lord's people— even if their culture says that it is a shameful thing to be a Christian.

 HAVE CONCERN FOR SINNERS

"What will become of the ungodly and the sinner?" (v 18).

The promise of the Lord's justice should comfort persecuted Christians. But equally, pray that this church would not be callous to those outside of it, but deeply concerned for their eternal future. Pray that they would be active in calling people to repentance and faith in the Lord Jesus.

 DO GOOD TO OTHERS

Thank God for the wonderful truth in verse 19: we have a "faithful Creator".

Pray that this assurance would liberate his people to "continue to do good". Pray that they'd be a blessing in their community as they do good deeds without expecting anything back; and that the way in which they repay good for evil would point others to the one true faithful Creator.

FOR...

THE UNREACHED

MATTHEW 9 v 35-38

PEOPLE TO PRAY FOR:

_____

_____

_____

_____

Whether they're in a far-flung country or a local council estate, pray for a specific "unreached" group:

GOOD NEWS FOR EVERYONE

Thank God that the news of Christ's kingdom is "good news" (v 35).

Praise God for the way that Jesus proclaimed it in "all the towns and villages"—no matter where or how people live, the gospel is universally good news. Thank God that he wants all nations and all types of people in his kingdom.

COMPASSION

People without Christ are "harassed and helpless"—and when Jesus was surrounded by the lost, "he had compassion" (v 36).

Yet when we contemplate the sheer number of lost people, often we can sink into indifference or apathetic hopelessness. Ask God to fill you with more of Christ's compassion. Ask him to make you faithful both in praying for the unreached, and in playing your part to reach them.

KNOW THE GOOD SHEPHERD

Thank Jesus that he is the good "shepherd" that people need (v 36).

Thank him for the way he laid down his life for his sheep; pray that many of these unreached people would come to understand the sacrifice of the cross. Pray that they'd experience the joy and security that comes from following the Good Shepherd.

PLENTIFUL HARVEST

It may not look this way, but Jesus is clear: "The harvest is plentiful" (v 37). Praise God!

Say sorry to God for the times when you've doubted this; for the times when—even unconsciously—you've dismissed people as too far, or too hard, or too messy. Ask him to encourage your soul with this truth: "The harvest is plentiful"!

SEND OUT MORE WORKERS

Jesus is equally clear that "the workers are few" (v 37).

And this is what he tells us to do about it: "Ask the Lord of the harvest, therefore, to send out workers into his harvest field" (v 38). So ask that now! And—if you dare!—ask God to use you as a worker in whatever part of his harvest field he wills.

EXPLORE THE WHOLE SERIES

"A THOUGHT-PROVOKING, VISION-EXPANDING, PRAYER-STIMULATING TOOL. SIMPLE, BUT BRILLIANT."

SINCLAIR FERGUSON

thegoodbook
COMPANY

BIBLICAL | RELEVANT | ACCESSIBLE

At The Good Book Company, we are dedicated to helping Christians and local churches grow. We believe that God's growth process always starts with hearing clearly what he has said to us through his timeless word—the Bible.

Ever since we opened our doors in 1991, we have been striving to produce Bible-based resources that bring glory to God. We have grown to become an international provider of user-friendly resources to the Christian community, with believers of all backgrounds and denominations using our books, Bible studies, devotionals, evangelistic resources, and DVD-based courses.

We want to equip ordinary Christians to live for Christ day by day, and churches to grow in their knowledge of God, their love for one another, and the effectiveness of their outreach.

Call us for a discussion of your needs or visit one of our local websites for more information on the resources and services we provide.

Your friends at The Good Book Company

thegoodbook.com | thegoodbook.co.uk
thegoodbook.com.au | thegoodbook.co.nz
thegoodbook.co.in